Garfield says a mouthful

BY: JIM DAVIS

BALLANTINE BOOKS · NEW YORK

Copyright © 1991 United Feature Syndicate, Inc.
GARFIELD Comic Strips: © 1990 United Feature Syndicate, Inc.

All rights reserved under International and Pan-American Copyright Conventions. Published in the United States by Ballantine Books, a division of Random House, Inc., New York, and simultaneously in Canada by Random House of Canada Limited, Toronto.

Library of Congress Catalog Card Number: 91-91856

ISBN: 0-345-37368-5

Manufactured in the United States of America

First Edition: October 1991

10 9 8 7 6 5 4 3 2

Top Ten Signs That Your Cat is a "Garfield"

10. Your food bill surpasses the national debt

9. He gets a court order requiring you to pamper him

8. He takes over everything in the house except the mortgage payment

7. Dogs in the neighborhood get anonymous hate mail

6. He has never strayed farther than three feet from the house

5. He treats you with no more respect than the drapes

4. Your plants die mysterious deaths

3. He's sometimes mistaken for Rhode Island

2. He tries to have *you* declawed

1. Can't tell if he's sleeping or dead

YOU GOTTA MAKE YOUR OWN FUN

JIM DAVIS 5-14

© 1990 United Feature Syndicate, Inc.

YES! IT IS I, BANANA MAN! HERE TO BRING HUMOR TO THE WORLD!

JUST SPREAD A FEW PEELS AROUND...

© 1990 United Feature Syndicate, Inc.

AND, VOILÀ! INSTANT FUN!

JIM DAVIS 5-15

WHY, JUST LOOK AT THAT GLOOMY FACE!

FEAR NOT! BANANA MAN IS HERE TO HELP!

WHY...WHY THANK YOU, BANANA MAN. I FEEL BETTER ALREADY!

JIM DAVIS 5-16

YIKES! ANOTHER DREARY, LISTLESS SOUL IN NEED OF ASSISTANCE

FROM...BANANA MAN!

MOO?

JIM DAVIS 5-17

© 1990 United Feature Syndicate, Inc.

SPLAT!

GARFIELD, YOU'RE CARRYING THIS BANANA THING TOO FAR!

THMILE WHEN YOU THAY THAT!

JIM DAVIS 5·18

GARFIELD! I'M SICK OF YOUR STUPID "BANANA MAN" ROUTINE! NOW FIND SOMETHING ELSE TO DO!

HI! I'M THE CHICKEN MAN, HERE TO ENTERTAIN YOU!

JIM DAVIS 5·19

CATS ARE ALWAYS UP TO SOMETHING...

SNEAKING AROUND THE HOUSE, CHASING RUBBER BALLS...

LEARNING TO USE THE CAN OPENER!

MY LIFE HAS NEW MEANING!

BRRRRR

JIM DAVIS 5-23

© 1990 United Feature Syndicate, Inc.

AND SO AS THE SUN GENTLY SETS...

WE PACK UP OUR MEMORIES...

AND BID FAREWELL TO OUR FIRST ANNUAL CHEESE FESTIVAL

JIM DAVIS 5-24

© 1990 United Feature Syndicate, Inc.

SIGH

LOOK AT ME, GARFIELD. I LOOK AWFUL

NO YOU DON'T

WHAT IF YOU GOT A FACE-LIFT?

AND A TUMMY TUCK

AND DIDN'T SLOUCH

JIM DAVIS 5-27

AND LOOSENED UP

© 1990 United Feature Syndicate, Inc.

NOW YOU LOOK AWFUL

"HAVE A CUP OF COFFEE, JON."
WHY, THANKS. DON'T MIND
IF I DO

JIM DAVIS 5-30

CONGRATULATIONS,
MR. ARBUCKLE

YOU ARE GOING TO GIVE BIRTH TO
A FINE, HEALTHY LITTER OF
PUPPIES

I
HATE
PUPPIES!

YOU HAVE THE MOST
BEWITCHING EYES...

JIM DAVIS 5-31

© 1990 United Feature Syndicate, Inc.

THEY CAST A
SPELL ON ME

WELL, IT'S NOT
WORKING

HOW
COME?

YOU'RE NOT A
SLUG YET

JiM DAViS 6·15

HOW WAS YOUR TENNIS DATE WITH GLORIA?

6·16

PTOOEY

SHE HAD A PRETTY GOOD SERVE

JiM DAViS

I AM PERSONALLY LOOKING FORWARD TO COLDER WEATHER

JIM DAVIS   6-20

HARK! A SAD FACE!

BANANA MAN TO THE RESCUE!

JIM DAVIS 6-21

© 1990 United Feature Syndicate, Inc.

♪ DING DONG

DING-DONG ♪

YAAAHH!

WHILE YOU'RE DOWN HERE, HOW ABOUT FILLING MY DISH?

GARFIELD

JIM DAVIS 6-24

HEY, GARFIELD! SPREAD OUT THE BLANKET, SET OUT LUNCH, TURN THE RADIO ON...

JIM DAVIS 6-29

AND SET UP THE UMBRELLA!

CHONK

© 1990 United Feature Syndicate, Inc.

AHH... I GUESS THE BEACH ISN'T SO BAD

JIM DAVIS

SLOOOSH!

© 1990 United Feature Syndicate, Inc.

IT'S WORSE

6-30

WAS THAT AN ECLIPSE?

OH, IT WAS JUST GARFIELD WALKING PAST THE WINDOW

SHADDUP

JIM DAVIS 7·4

IT'S IMPOSSIBLE NOT TO ENJOY THE PLAYFUL NATURE OF A CAT

JIM DAVIS 7·5

HEY, GARFIELD. LET'S HAVE SOME FUN!

DO YOU HAVE AN APPOINTMENT?

I CONFESS!

I'VE BEEN PLOTTING TO STEAL YOUR CANDY BAR!

THAT'S A LOAD OFF THE OL' CONSCIENCE

JIM DAVIS 7-6

© 1990 United Feature Syndicate, Inc.

THE SECRET TO CATCHING BIRDS IS PATIENCE

UH... GARFIELD

SHHH!

JIM DAVIS 7-7

© 1990 United Feature Syndicate, Inc.

THE SINK'S OVERFLOWING!

WELL BAIL IT OUT

YOU CLOGGED IT UP WITH YOUR STUPID CAT HAIR!

EXCUSE ME FOR BEING A CAT

JIM DAVIS 78

I DON'T HAVE TO TAKE THIS

© 1990 United Feature Syndicate, Inc.

I'M GOING TO STAND OUT HERE, IN THE RAIN, TILL JON APOLOGIZES

CLICK

AH, HE'S COME TO HIS SENSES

GOOSH!

© 1990 United Feature Syndicate, Inc.

YAWN

TIME FOR BED

WHAT TH-?!

Z

OKAY, ODIE. COME OUT AND FACE THE MUSIC!

POKE POKE

CUT IT OUT. I'M TRYING TO GET SOME SLEEP HERE

SCORE ONE FOR THE BIG GUY

JIM DAVIS 8-5

IMPRESSIONS

MONA LISA

JiM DAVis 8-6

IMPRESSIONS

A TURTLE!

JiM DAVis 8-7

© 1990 United Feature Syndicate, Inc.

TIME FOR YOUR BRUSHING, GARFIELD

JIM DAVIS 8-12

COME HERE!

NOW HOLD STILL!

BRUSH BRUSH BRUSH BRUSH
BRUSH BRUSH
BRUSH
BRUSH
BRUSH
BRUSH

© 1990 United Feature Syndicate, Inc.

DOC! YOU GOTTA HELP MY CAT!

 WHAT AN AWFUL SHOW

 THERE HAS TO BE SOMETHING BETTER ON THAN THIS!... WHERE'S THAT REMOTE CONTROL?

 UMFFFF

 EEERRRGGGH

 NNNGGGHHHH

 ACTUALLY, IT ISN'T THAT AWFUL

AND NOW... INN-TRO-DUCING... GARFIELD, THE AMAZING!!!

TAH-DAHHHH!

...NOTHING UP MY SUPPER DISH...
SNIFF SNIFF

TAP TAP TAP

HMM

SNIP SNIP

COUPON FOR CAT FOOD

GUESS HOW MANY BALL BEARINGS FIT IN YOUR SOCKS?

RiiiP!

THAT MANY

WHICH WOULD YOU RATHER DO, GARFIELD, GO TO THE FARM, OR GO CAMPING?

© 1990 United Feature Syndicate, Inc.

WOULD HAVING SOMETHING AMPUTATED BE A CHOICE?

JIM DAVIS 9-17

BOY, IT'S COLD! I CAN HARDLY WAIT TO TRY OUT MY NEW ELECTRIC SOCKS!

8   9-18

WHERE'D THEY GO?!

JIM DAVIS

NOTHING LIKE A HOT SOCK OF COFFEE IN THE MORNING, HUH, ODIE?

SLOOK

© 1990 United Feature Syndicate, Inc.

© 1990 United Feature Syndicate, Inc.

JIM DAVIS 9-23

PUNT!

FOOF!

PLPLPLPLPL

© 1990 United Feature Syndicate, Inc.

JIM DAVIS 9-28

THIS IS THE LAST CUP OF COFFEE IN THE HOUSE

JIM DAVIS 9-29

CLAWS ON A CHALKBOARD!

© 1990 United Feature Syndicate, Inc.

AND YOU MAY HAVE IT

WHY, THANK YOU!

© 1990 United Feature Syndicate, Inc.

AND I USED TO HATE GETTING UP IN THE MORNING

CRUNCH CRUNCH CRUNCH

I LOVE OBSERVING SPIDERS

WHAP!

THEY'RE EASIER TO OBSERVE IF THEY'RE STANDING STILL

I'VE TAUGHT ODIE A NEW TRICK

POOMP

DOWN, BOY!

GOOD BOY!

JIM DAVIS 10-12

© 1990 United Feature Syndicate, Inc.

HERE'S A PHOTO OF MY DAD

ALBUM

"A GOOD FARMER HAS A SENSE OF HUMOR," HE ALWAYS SAYS

THAT EXPLAINS THE CORNCOB IN THE EAR

JIM DAVIS 10-13

© 1990 United Feature Syndicate, Inc.

POOMP!

IS IT JUST ME? OR IS EVERYBODY IN A BAD MOOD TODAY?

JIM DAVIS 10-15

UH-OH, HERE COMES THE SCOUT

HERE COMES THE ARMY

JIM DAVIS 10-16

AND THERE GOES THE CHUCK WAGON

GARFIELD!

STUPID CLAWS

HERE I SIT, WASTING TIME WATCHING TELEVISION

WHILE OTHERS ARE BUCKLING DOWN, WORKING HARD AND GETTING THINGS DONE

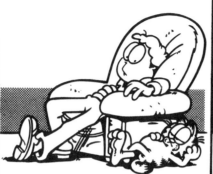

© 1990 United Feature Syndicate, Inc.

10-21   JIM DAVIS

ANY IDEA WHERE THESE COOKIES WENT?

© 1990 United Feature Syndicate, Inc.

WELL?!

FOR A CAT WHO WALKS ON HIS HIND LEGS, YOU DON'T TALK MUCH!

JIM DAVIS 10·26

SIGH...

JIM DAVIS 10·27

© 1990 United Feature Syndicate, Inc.

ONLY YOU, GARFIELD...

ONLY YOU COULD GIVE A TIRE SWING A FLAT

MAYBE IT HAD A SLOW LEAK

OKAY, ODIE, THIS TIME YOU'RE GOING CLEAR THROUGH THE CEILING!

...CLEAR TO THE MOON!

JIM DAVIS 11-4   © 1990 United Feature Syndicate, Inc.

...THE HECK WITH THE MOON... CLEAR INTO OUTER SPACE!

AAARRRGGGHHH!

CLICK

THAT'S IT! I'M TIRED OF US NEVER AGREEING ON WHICH TV SHOW TO WATCH

YOU CAN WATCH THE BEDROOM TV AND I'LL WATCH THE LIVING ROOM TV

© 1990 United Feature Syndicate, Inc.

LOOK AT THESE FOOD SPOTS ON MY TIE. THIS IS A GRAVY STAIN

© 1990 United Feature Syndicate, Inc.

AND I CAN'T REMEMBER WHAT THIS ONE IS

APPLE COBBLER... WITH VANILLA ICE CREAM... A LITTLE HEAVY ON THE CINNAMON

I'M GOING TO CLEAN THE REFRIGERATOR

I'LL HELP

© 1990 United Feature Syndicate, Inc.

LET'S SEE IF I HAVE EVERYTHING... RUBBER GLOVES, TRASH BAGS, SCOURING PAD...

GOGGLES, FLAME THROWER...

JIM DAVIS 11-15

© 1990 United Feature Syndicate, Inc.

JiM DAViS 11-25

JON'S SODA POP!

SHAKE SHAKE SHAKE SHAKE SHAKE SHAKE SHAKE

AH-HA!

HE THINKS I'M GOING TO OPEN THIS AND SPRAY SODA POP IN MY FACE

WELL, WE'LL JUST SEE WHO HAS THE LAST LAUGH!

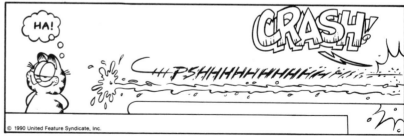

HA!

CRASH!

PSHHHHHHHHHH

JIM DAVIS 12-2

© 1990 United Feature Syndicate, Inc.

GARFIELD'S TOP TEN NIGHTMARES

10. **NERMAL GETS CLONED**

9. **VET PRESCRIBES "CHAIN SAW THERAPY"**

8. **FALLS INTO VAT OF ODIE DROOL**

7. **FLEAS VOTE HIM "MOST BLOODSUCKABLE"**

6. **MISTAKES JON'S SWEAT SOCK FOR A MATZOH BALL**

5. **FORCED TO WATCH THE "ALL LASSIE" CHANNEL**

4. **TRAPPED FOR A WEEK INSIDE HEALTH FOOD STORE**

3. **CAT FUR BECOMES THE LATEST THING FOR WOMEN'S COATS**

2. **MEETS HUGE SPIDER WITH AN ATTITUDE**

1. **DIET MONDAY!**

STRIPS, SPECIALS OR BESTSELLING BOOKS...
GARFIELD'S ON EVERYONE'S MENU

Don't miss even one episode in the Tubby Tabby's hilarious series!

___GARFIELD AT LARGE (#1)   32013/$6.95
___GARFIELD GAINS WEIGHT (#2)   32008/$6.95
___GARFIELD BIGGER THAN LIFE (#3)   32007/$6.95
___GARFIELD WEIGHS IN (#4)   32010/$6.95
___GARFIELD TAKES THE CAKE (#5)   32009/$6.95
___GARFIELD EATS HIS HEART OUT (#6)   32018/$6.95
___GARFIELD SITS AROUND THE HOUSE (#7)   32011/$6.95
___GARFIELD TIPS THE SCALE (#8)   33580/$6.95
___GARFIELD LOSES HIS FEET (#9)   31805/$6.95
___GARFIELD MAKES IT BIG (#10)   31928/$6.95
___GARFIELD ROLLS ON (#11)   32634/$6.95
___GARFIELD OUT TO LUNCH (#12)   33118/$6.95
___GARFIELD FOOD FOR THOUGHT (#13)   34129/$6.95

___GARFIELD SWALLOWS HIS PRIDE (#14)   34725/$6.95
___GARFIELD WORLDWIDE (#15)   35158/$6.95
___GARFIELD ROUNDS OUT (#16)   35388/$6.95
___GARFIELD CHEWS THE FAT (#17)   35956/$6.95
___GARFIELD GOES TO WAIST (#18)   36430/$6.95
___GARFIELD HANGS OUT (#19)   36835/$6.95
___GARFIELD TAKES UP SPACE (#20)   37029/$6.95
___GARFIELD SAYS A MOUTHFUL (#21)   37368/$6.95

GARFIELD AT HIS SUNDAY BEST!
___GARFIELD TREASURY   33106/$9.95
___THE SECOND GARFIELD TREASURY   33276/$10.95
___THE THIRD GARFIELD TREASURY   32635/$9.95
___THE FOURTH GARFIELD TREASURY   34726/$10.95
___THE FIFTH GARFIELD TREASURY   36268/$9.95
___THE SIXTH GARFIELD TREASURY   37367/$10.95

BALLANTINE SALES
Dept. TA, 201 E. 50th St., New York, N.Y. 10022

Please send me the BALLANTINE BOOKS I have checked above. I am enclosing $ .... (add $2.00 for the first book and 50¢ for each additional book to cover postage and handling). Send check or money order—no cash or C.O.D.'s please. Prices are subject to change without notice.

Name _____

Address _____

City _____ State _____ Zip Code _____

30   Allow at least 4 weeks for delivery   3/90 TA-135